MAD's

LOOKS AT OUR
PLANET

D1716165

WARNER BOOKS

A Time Warner Company

WARNER BOOKS EDITION

This Warner Books Edition is published by arrangement with E.C. Publications, Inc.

Warner Books, Inc.
666 Fifth Avenue
New York, N.Y. 10103

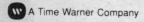 A Time Warner Company

Printed in the United States of America

First Printing: April, 1986

Reissued: August, 1991

10 9 8 7 6 5 4 3 2

WEIRD ARTIFACTS OF OUR PLANET

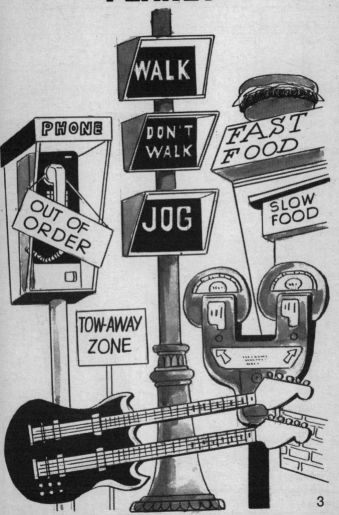

5

SEEN BUT NOT HURT

Doctor, I'm such a klutz. I'm always tripping over things and **hurting** myself. I've got a pain in my **back,** a pain in my right **arm,** and a pain in my **neck.**

①

Maybe your **coordination** is off. Let me check your **reflexes.**

6

②

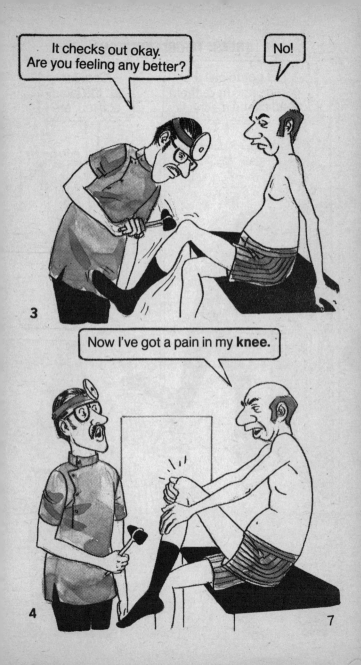

9

11

13

HOOK LINE AND SINK HER

17

3

19

21

WEDDING NOT

25

27

CHOW HOUNDED

29

LOOKS ARE SKIM DEEP

31

FLIGHT FRIGHT

32

33

35

37

DOWN FOR THE COUNT

38

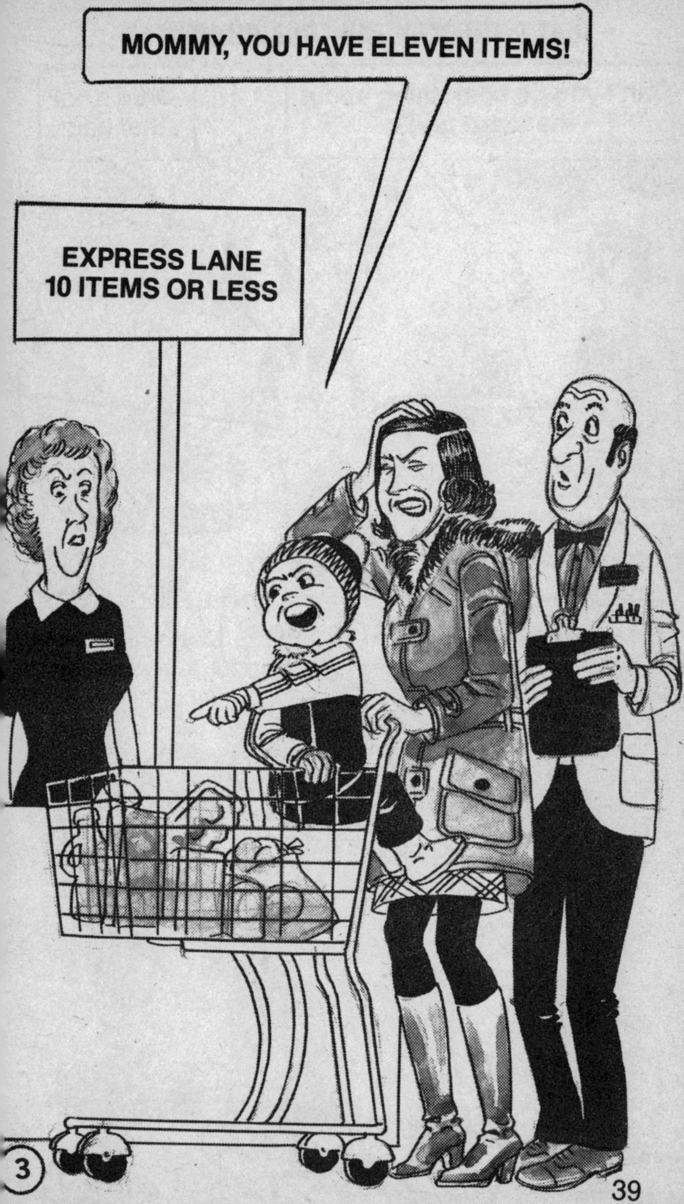
MOMMY, YOU HAVE ELEVEN ITEMS!
EXPRESS LANE
10 ITEMS OR LESS

THAT'S THE WAY THE COOK CRUMBLES

40

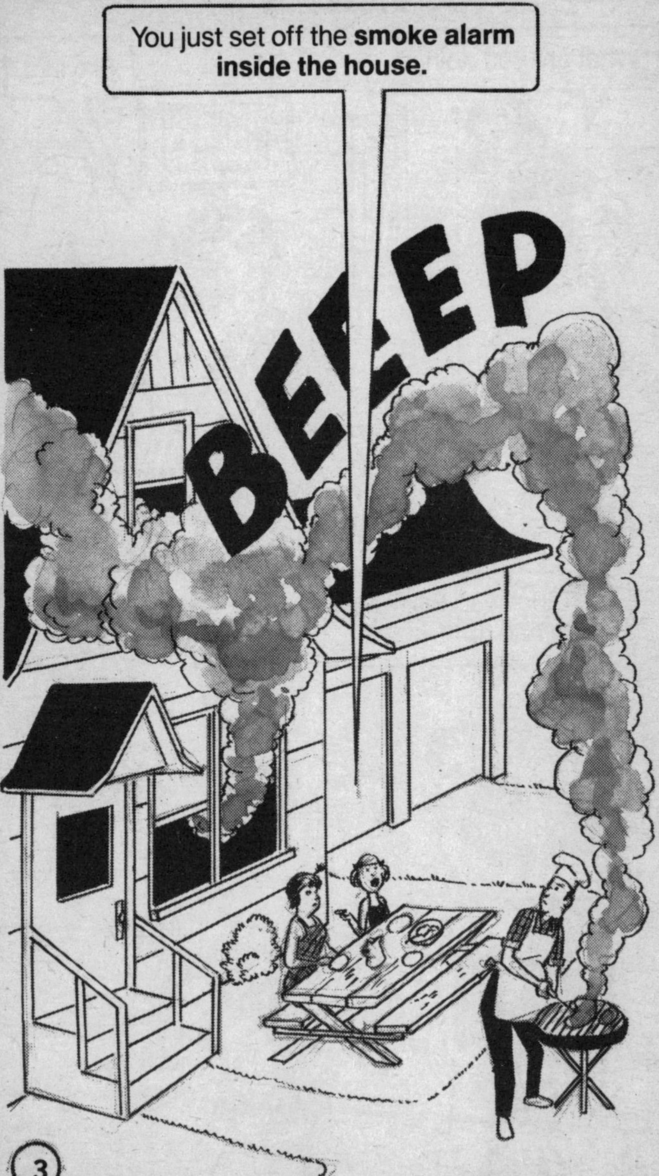

3

GROWING PAIN

43

DELIVERING THE MALE

44

45

BILLING AND STEWING

47

LOUD AND UNCLEAR

49

TRIPS THAT PASS IN THE NIGHT

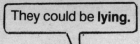

51

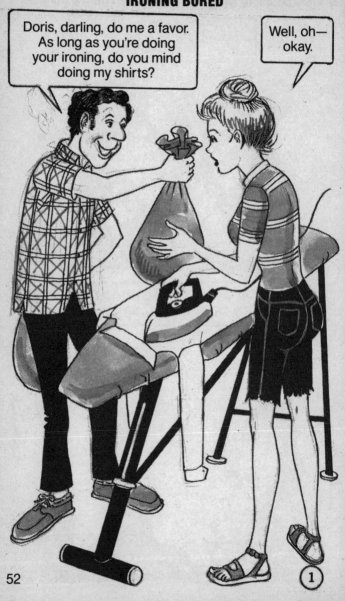

53

CALL GIRLS

54

POWER SOURCE

57

HANG-UPS

59

61

WEATHER OR NOT

Oh, my, it's **raining** pretty hard outside. You better dress accordingly.

①

Okay, you're all set. You've got on your raincoat and boots. Most important of all, here is the **umbrella. Use it!**

Honest, Mom, everytime you give me the umbrella, I make good use of it going to and from school.

②

63

POUND FOOLISH

65

MODERN WHIRLED

It's no use. I can't cope with **modern technology.**

What are you talking about? You **graduated college Phi Beta Kappa.** You have a very **responsible** job.

67

WHO'S COUNTING

WEIRD CREATURES THAT INHABIT OUR PLANET

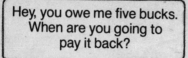

71

BATTLE WARY

79

SCHOOL DAZE

I'll have to go back again tomorrow.

81

83

PAIN IN THE CLASS

I'm Cliff Miller's mother. How's my son doing in school?

Oh yes, good ol' Cliff the **hyperkinetic** child with boundless energy—probably caused by eating too much sugary food.

He doesn't sit still for a minute. He's all over the place. He doesn't pay too much attention to class work. He's constantly talking and in general disrupts the whole class.

85

BABY TALK

②

91

FUSS BUDGET

92

(3)

(4)

93

95

PENNIES FROM HEAVEN

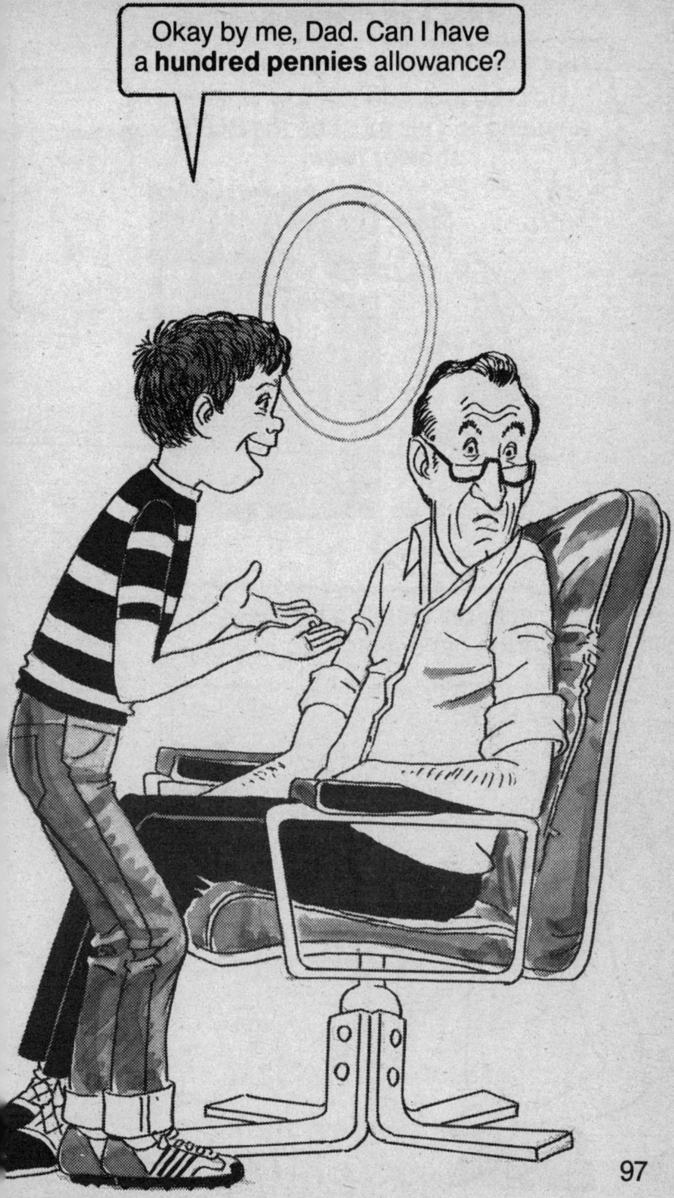
Okay by me, Dad. Can I have a **hundred pennies** allowance?

98

ALL BETS ARE OFF

101

NOTHING IS FOR NOTHING

105

107

I'm sorry to be a tattletale. But I saw your boyfriend **Mitch** out with **Nancy Pumpernickel.**

I saw it too.

So did I.

①

Okay, Buster, just what's going on between you and Nancy Pumpernickel?

Nothing. We **accidentally** met at Burger King and we shared a table. **That's all.**

108

②

THE HIGH COST OF LEAVING

111

Things get **marked down** after the **holidays.**

113

BYE LINGUAL

Michael is studying **French** and **biology** in school and doing **marvelously** in both subjects.

(1)

Michael, say **"Good day"** to your grandmother in **French.**

Bon jour!

114

(2)

WORLDLY WISE

CHANGING WHIRLED

Let's go shopping or something.

I don't know if I'm up to it.

This morning I had my hair dyed **blond.** I took a sunbath to make my skin **tanner,** I'm wearing a padded bra to make me look **fuller.** I'm wearing a girdle to make me look **thinner,** and platform shoes to make me look **taller.**

119

121

WINNING BY A NO'S

123

SLEEPY-TIME PAL

125

DOWN MEMORY SLAIN

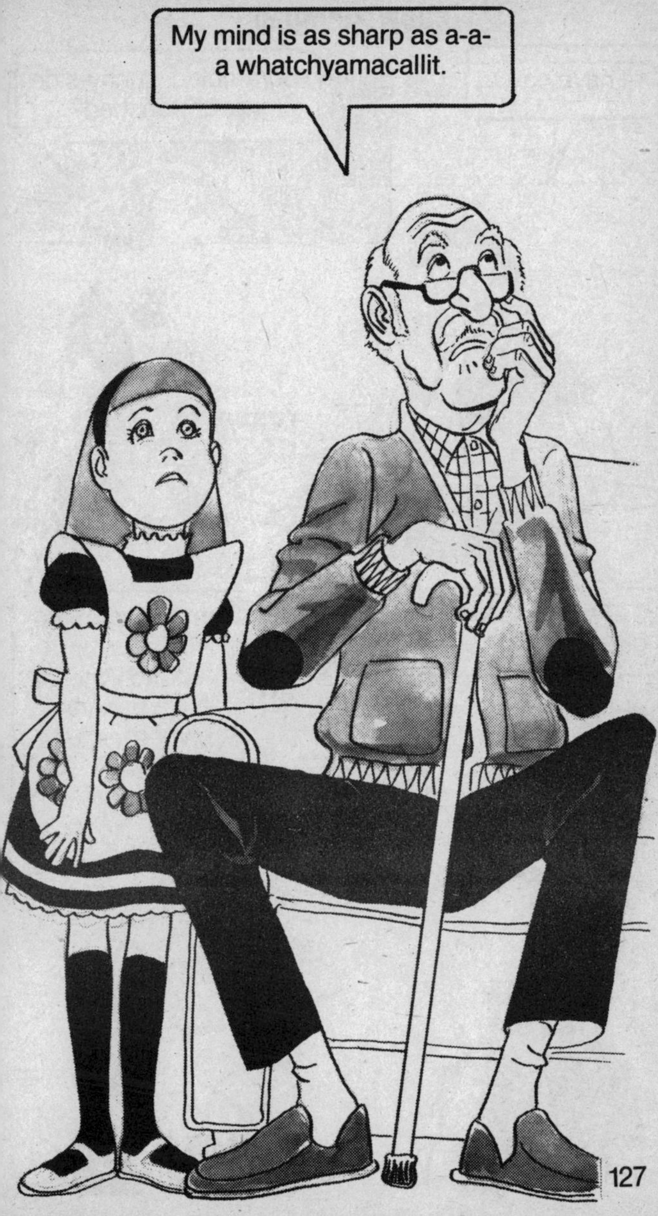
My mind is as sharp as a-a-
a whatchyamacallit.

CHOW HOUNDED

129

130

...But my **teacher** always **beats me to it.**

131

FOOD FOR NAUGHT

133

THAT'S PARK FOR THE COURSE

THE HOLE TRUTH

136

WATER LOGGED

139

COME AND FORGET IT

141

FORE PLAY

143

COMMUNICATE SHUN

144

145

THE RACE IS NOT ALWAYS TO THE SWIFT

Nancy, why did you hit Bruce?

So he'll run after me!

149

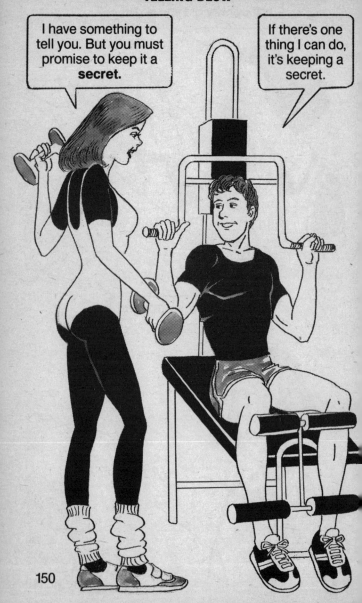

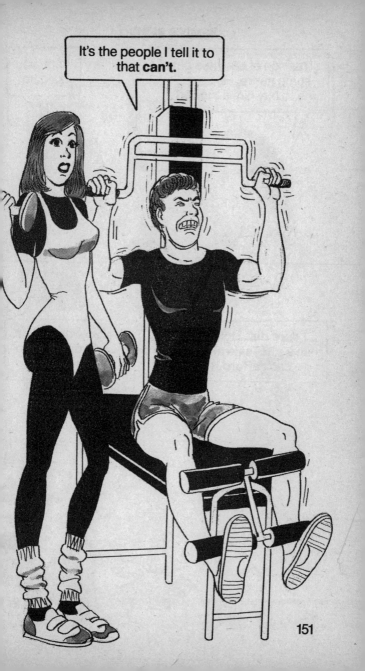

151

HEAVEN BENT

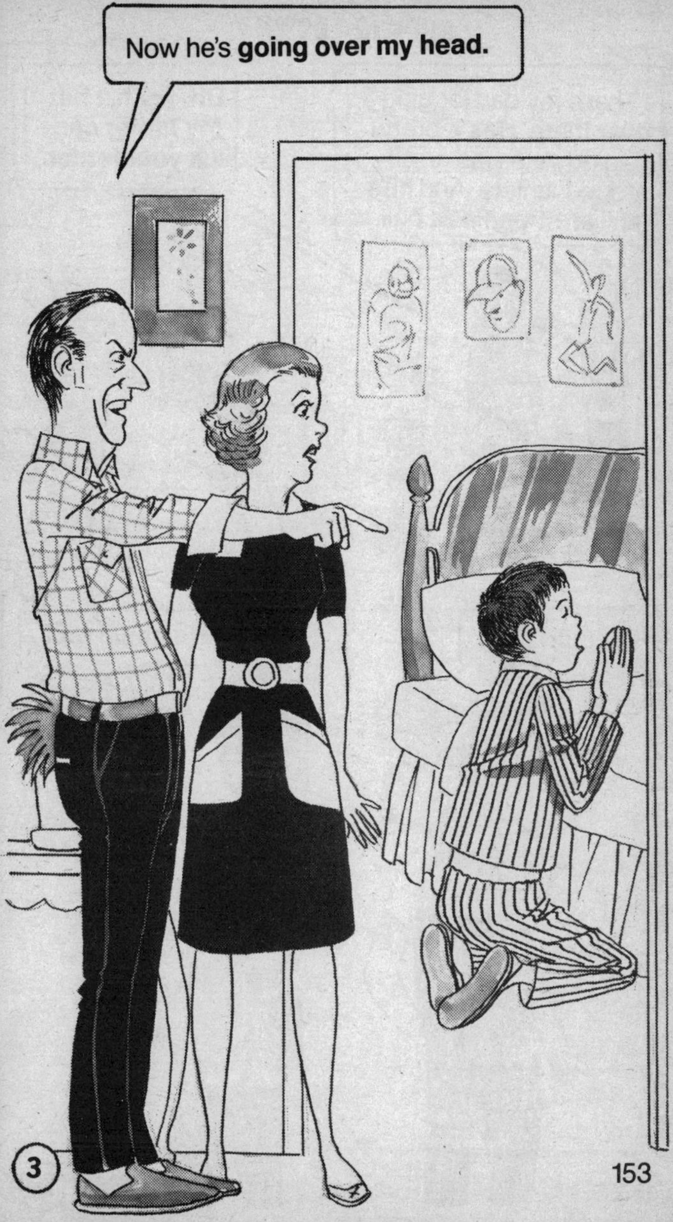
Now he's going over my head.
3

GROWING DOWN

155

THINK OR SWIM

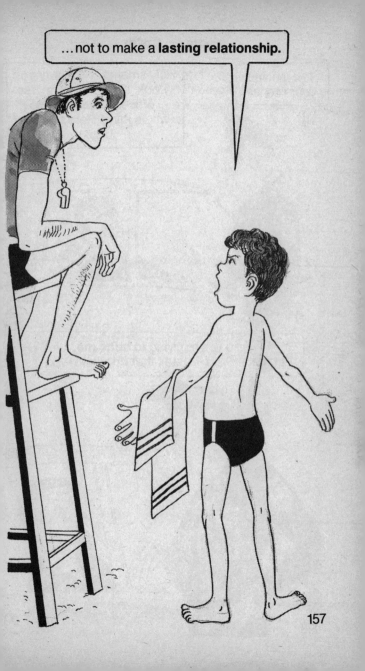

157

COPPING A PLEA

159

Oh really? Then tell me, my **baseball-fanatic** son, what is the **last line** of **"The Star-Spangled Banner?"**
3

"PLAY BALL!"
4

HOME OF THE RAVE

Home to me means warmth, love, and security. No matter how long I've been away, or how late I come home, **there's always a light burning for me in the window:**

PET PEEVE

Happy Birthday to you,
Happy Birthday to you,
Happy Birthday, dear Fido,
Happy Birthday to you.

①

And here's the fancy-shmancy
birthday cake that Mom made for you.

②

165

ON THE JOB STRAINING

166

167

169

RELATIONSLIP

170

171

173

PARDON MY WRENCH

175

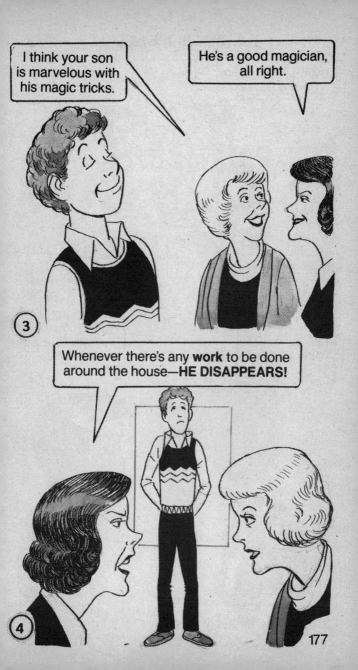

177

RING IN THE NO'S

178

KIN AND BEAR IT

A TALE OF TWO WITTIES

Hey, gorgeous, I heard this real great **dirty story**.

So did I. Let me tell you mine first.

①

There was this real sexy secretary. One day her boss told her a real dirty filthy embarrassingly bad-taste story.

②

183

There is Sandy Dunk.
He's the **smartest** student in the class. He's **always** reading ...

...even when he's **not** in the **bathroom**.

185

GONE WITH THE WHINE

187

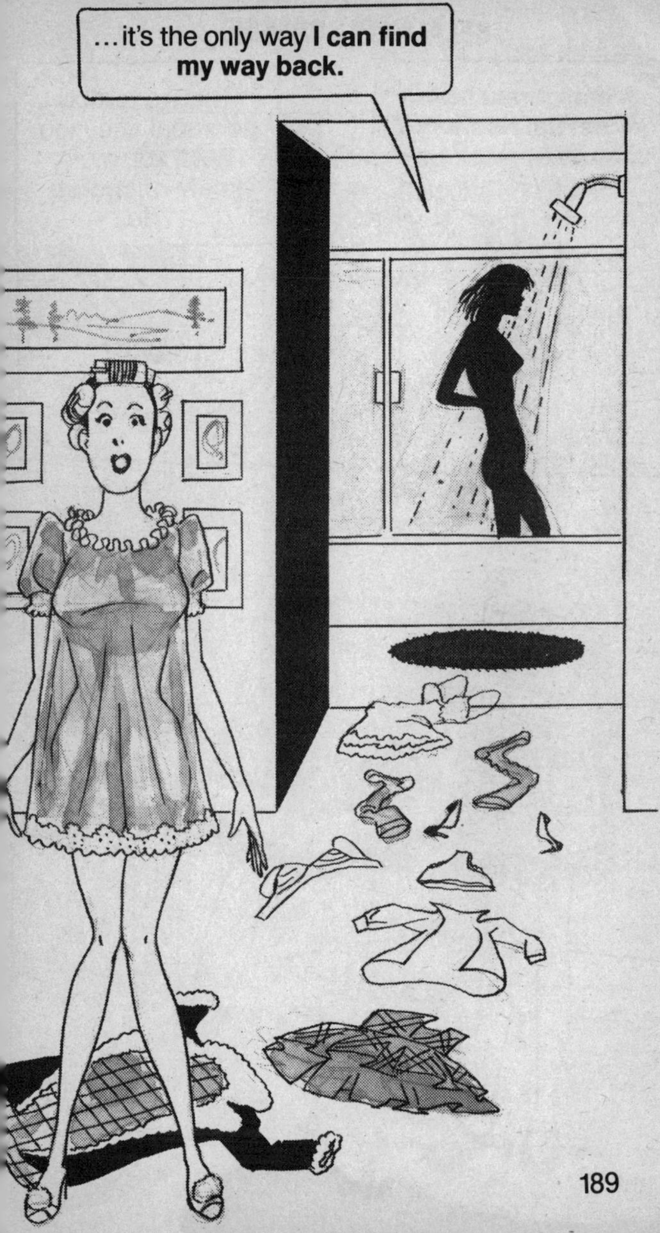
...it's the only way I can find my way back.

So how come you never introduced me to **that side of the family?**
David Berg